Love Poems and Others

Love Poems and Others

D.H. Lawrence

MINT EDITIONS

Love Poems and Others was first published in 1913.

This edition published by Mint Editions 2021.

ISBN 9781513270524 | E-ISBN 9781513275529

Published by Mint Editions®

MINT EDITIONS
minteditionbooks.com

Publishing Director: Jennifer Newens
Design & Production: Rachel Lopez Metzger
Typesetting: Westchester Publishing Services

Contents

LOVE POEMS

I

Wedding Morn

The morning breaks like a pomegranate
    In a shining crack of red,
Ah, when to-morrow the dawn comes late
    Whitening across the bed,
It will find me watching at the marriage gate
    And waiting while light is shed
On him who is sleeping satiate,
    With a sunk, abandoned head.

And when the dawn comes creeping in,
    Cautiously I shall raise
Myself to watch the morning win
    My first of days,
As it shows him sleeping a sleep he got
    Of me, as under my gaze,
He grows distinct, and I see his hot
    Face freed of the wavering blaze.

Then I shall know which image of God
    My man is made toward,
And I shall know my bitter rod
    Or my rich reward.
And I shall know the stamp and worth
    Of the coin I've accepted as mine,
Shall see an image of heaven or of earth
    On his minted metal shine.

Yea and I long to see him sleep
    In my power utterly,
I long to know what I have to keep,
    I long to see
My love, that spinning coin, laid still
    And plain at the side of me,

For me to count—for I know he will
    Greatly enrichen me.

And then he will be mine, he will lie
    In my power utterly,
Opening his value plain to my eye
    He will sleep of me.
He will lie negligent, resign
    His all to me, and I
Shall watch the dawn light up for me
    This sleeping wealth of mine.

And I shall watch the wan light shine
    On his sleep that is filled of me,
On his brow where the wisps of fond hair twine
    So truthfully,
On his lips where the light breaths come and go
    Naïve and winsomely,
On his limbs that I shall weep to know
    Lie under my mastery.

D.H. LAWRENCE

Kisses in the Train

I saw the midlands
    Revolve through her hair;
The fields of autumn
    Stretching bare,
And sheep on the pasture
    Tossed back in a scare.

And still as ever
    The world went round,
My mouth on her pulsing
    Neck was found,
And my breast to her beating
    Breast was bound.

But my heart at the centre
    Of all, in a swound
Was still as a pivot,
    As all the ground
On its prowling orbit
    Shifted round.

And still in my nostrils
    The scent of her flesh,
And still my wet mouth
    Sought her afresh;
And still one pulse
    Through the world did thresh.

And the world all whirling
    Around in joy
Like the dance of a dervish
    Did destroy

My sense—and my reason
    Spun like a toy.

But firm at the centre
    My heart was found;
Her own to my perfect
    Heart-beat bound,
Like a magnet's keeper
    Closing the round.

III

CRUELTY AND LOVE

What large, dark hands are those at the window
Lifted, grasping the golden light
Which weaves its way through the creeper leaves
    To my heart's delight?

Ah, only the leaves! But in the west,
In the west I see a redness come
Over the evening's burning breast—
    —'Tis the wound of love goes home!

 The woodbine creeps abroad
 Calling low to her lover:
  The sun-lit flirt who all the day
  Has poised above her lips in play
  And stolen kisses, shallow and gay
  Of pollen, now has gone away
  —She woos the moth with her sweet, low word,
 And when above her his broad wings hover
 Then her bright breast she will uncover
 And yield her honey-drop to her lover.

 Into the yellow, evening glow
 Saunters a man from the farm below,
 Leans, and looks in at the low-built shed
 Where hangs the swallow's marriage bed.
  The bird lies warm against the wall.
  She glances quick her startled eyes
  Towards him, then she turns away
  Her small head, making warm display
  Of red upon the throat. His terrors sway
  Her out of the nest's warm, busy ball,
  Whose plaintive cry is heard as she flies
  In one blue stoop from out the sties
  Into the evening's empty hall.

Oh, water-hen, beside the rushes
Hide your quaint, unfading blushes,
Still your quick tail, and lie as dead,
Till the distance folds over his ominous tread.

The rabbit presses back her ears,
Turns back her liquid, anguished eyes
And crouches low: then with wild spring
Spurts from the terror of *his* oncoming
To be choked back, the wire ring
Her frantic effort throttling:
     Piteous brown ball of quivering fears!

Ah soon in his large, hard hands she dies,
And swings all loose to the swing of his walk.
Yet calm and kindly are his eyes
And ready to open in brown surprise
Should I not answer to his talk
Or should he my tears surmise.

I hear his hand on the latch, and rise from my chair
Watching the door open: he flashes bare
His strong teeth in a smile, and flashes his eyes
In a smile like triumph upon me; then careless-wise
He flings the rabbit soft on the table board
And comes towards me: ah, the uplifted sword
Of his hand against my bosom, and oh, the broad
Blade of his hand that raise my face to applaud
His coming: he raises up my face to him
And caresses my mouth with his fingers, which still smell grim
Of the rabbit's fur! God, I am caught in a snare!
I know not what fine wire is round my throat,
I only know I let him finger there
My pulse of life, letting him nose like a stoat
Who sniffs with joy before he drinks the blood:
And down his mouth comes to my mouth, and down
His dark bright eyes descend like a fiery hood
Upon my mind: his mouth meets mine, and a flood
Of sweet fire sweeps across me, so I drown
Within him, die, and find death good.

          D.H. LAWRENCE

IV

Cherry Robbers

Under the long, dark boughs, like jewels red
     In the hair of an Eastern girl
Shine strings of crimson cherries, as if had bled
     Blood-drops beneath each curl.

Under the glistening cherries, with folded wings
     Three dead birds lie:
Pale-breasted throstles and a blackbird, robberlings
     Stained with red dye.

Under the haystack a girl stands laughing at me,
     With cherries hung round her ears—
Offering me her scarlet fruit: I will see
     If she has any tears.

V

Lilies in the Fire

I

Ah, you stack of white lilies, all white and gold,
I am adrift as a sunbeam, and without form
Or having, save I light on you to warm
Your pallor into radiance, flush your cold

White beauty into incandescence: you
Are not a stack of white lilies to-night, but a white
And clustered star transfigured by me to-night,
And lighting these ruddy leaves like a star dropped through

The slender bare arms of the branches, your tire-maidens
Who lift swart arms to fend me off; but I come
Like a wind of fire upon you, like to some
Stray whitebeam who on you his fire unladens.

And you are a glistening toadstool shining here
Among the crumpled beech-leaves phosphorescent,
My stack of white lilies burning incandescent
Of me, a soft white star among the leaves, my dear.

II

Is it with pain, my dear, that you shudder so?
Is it because I have hurt you with pain, my dear?

Did I shiver?—Nay, truly I did not know—
A dewdrop may-be splashed on my face down here.

Why even now you speak through close-shut teeth.
I have been too much for you—Ah, I remember!

D.H. LAWRENCE

The ground is a little chilly underneath
The leaves—and, dear, you consume me all to an ember.

You hold yourself all hard as if my kisses
Hurt as I gave them—you put me away—

    Ah never I put you away: yet each kiss hisses
    Hot as a drop of fire wastes me away.

III

I am ashamed, you wanted me not to-night—
Nay, it is always so, you sigh with me.
Your radiance dims when I draw too near, and my free
Fire enters your petals like death, you wilt dead white.

Ah, I do know, and I am deep ashamed;
You love me while I hover tenderly
Like clinging sunbeams kissing you: but see
When I close in fire upon you, and you are flamed

With the swiftest fire of my love, you are destroyed.
'Tis a degradation deep to me, that my best
Soul's whitest lightning which should bright attest
God stepping down to earth in one white stride,

Means only to you a clogged, numb burden of flesh
Heavy to bear, even heavy to uprear
Again from earth, like lilies wilted and sere
Flagged on the floor, that before stood up so fresh.

VI

COLDNESS IN LOVE

And you remember, in the afternoon
The sea and the sky went grey, as if there had sunk
A flocculent dust on the floor of the world: the festoon
Of the sky sagged dusty as spider cloth,
And coldness clogged the sea, till it ceased to croon.

A dank, sickening scent came up from the grime
Of weed that blackened the shore, so that I recoiled
Feeling the raw cold dun me: and all the time
You leapt about on the slippery rocks, and threw
The words that rang with a brassy, shallow chime.

And all day long that raw and ancient cold
Deadened me through, till the grey downs darkened to sleep.
Then I longed for you with your mantle of love to fold
Me over, and drive from out of my body the deep
Cold that had sunk to my soul, and there kept hold.

But still to me all evening long you were cold,
And I was numb with a bitter, deathly ache;
Till old days drew me back into their fold,
And dim sheep crowded me warm with companionship,
And old ghosts clustered me close, and sleep was cajoled.

I slept till dawn at the window blew in like dust,
Like the linty, raw-cold dust disturbed from the floor
Of a disused room: a grey pale light like must
That settled upon my face and hands till it seemed
To flourish there, as pale mould blooms on a crust.

Then I rose in fear, needing you fearfully,
For I thought you were warm as a sudden jet of blood.
I thought I could plunge in your spurting hotness, and be

Clean of the cold and the must.—With my hand on the latch
I heard you in your sleep speak strangely to me.

And I dared not enter, feeling suddenly dismayed.
So I went and washed my deadened flesh in the sea
And came back tingling clean, but worn and frayed
With cold, like the shell of the moon: and strange it seems
That my love has dawned in rose again, like the love of a maid.

VII

End of another Home-Holiday

I

When shall I see the half moon sink again
Behind the black sycamore at the end of the garden?
When will the scent of the dim, white phlox
Creep up the wall to me, and in at my open window?

Why is it, the long slow stroke of the midnight bell,
  (Will it never finish the twelve?)
Falls again and again on my heart with a heavy reproach?

The moon-mist is over the village, out of the mist speaks the bell,
And all the little roofs of the village bow low, pitiful, beseeching, resigned:
  Oh, little home, what is it I have not done well?

Ah home, suddenly I love you,
As I hear the sharp clean trot of a pony down the road,
Succeeding sharp little sounds dropping into the silence,
Clear upon the long-drawn hoarseness of a train across the valley.

The light has gone out from under my mother's door.
    That she should love me so,
    She, so lonely, greying now,
    And I leaving her,
    Bent on my pursuits!

  Love is the great Asker,
  The sun and the rain do not ask the secret

Of the time when the grain struggles down in the dark.
The moon walks her lonely way without anguish,
Because no loved one grieves over her departure.

II

Forever, ever by my shoulder pitiful Love will linger,
Crouching as little houses crouch under the mist when I turn.
Forever, out of the mist the church lifts up her reproachful finger,
Pointing my eyes in wretched defiance where love hides her face to
mourn.

    Oh but the rain creeps down to wet the grain
        That struggles alone in the dark,
    And asking nothing, cheerfully steals back again!
        The moon sets forth o' nights
        To walk the lonely, dusky heights
        Serenely, with steps unswerving;
        Pursued by no sigh of bereavement,
        No tears of love unnerving
        Her constant tread:
    While ever at my side,
        Frail and sad, with grey bowed head,
        The beggar-woman, the yearning-eyed
        Inexorable love goes lagging.

The wild young heifer, glancing distraught,
With a strange new knocking of life at her side
    Runs seeking a loneliness.
The little grain draws down the earth to hide.
Nay, even the slumberous egg, as it labours under the shell,
    Patiently to divide, and self-divide,
Asks to be hidden, and wishes nothing to tell.

But when I draw the scanty cloak of silence over my eyes,
Piteous Love comes peering under the hood.
Touches the clasp with trembling fingers, and tries
To put her ear to the painful sob of my blood,
While her tears soak through to my breast,
      Where they burn and cauterise.

III

The moon lies back and reddens.
In the valley, a corncrake calls
    Monotonously,
With a piteous, unalterable plaint, that deadens
    My confident activity:
With a hoarse, insistent request that falls
    Unweariedly, unweariedly,
    Asking something more of me,
    Yet more of me!

VIII

Reminder

Do you remember
How night after night swept level and low
Overhead, at home, and had not one star,
Nor one narrow gate for the moon to go
     Forth to her field of November.

And you remember,
How towards the north a red blot on the sky
Burns like a blotch of anxiety
Over the forges, and small flames ply
     Like ghosts the shadow of the ember.

Those were the days
When it was awful autumn to me,
When only there glowed on the dark of the sky
The red reflection of her agony,
     My beloved smelting down in the blaze

Of death—my dearest
Love who had borne, and was now leaving me.
And I at the foot of her cross did suffer
     My own gethsemane.

So I came to you,
And twice, after great kisses, I saw
The rim of the moon divinely rise
And strive to detach herself from the raw
     Blackened edge of the skies.

Strive to escape;
With her whiteness revealing my sunken world
Tall and loftily shadowed. But the moon
Never magnolia-like unfurled
     Her white, her lamp-like shape.

For you told me no,
And bade me not to ask for the dour
Communion, offering—"a better thing."
So I lay on your breast for an obscure hour
      Feeling your fingers go

      Like a rhythmic breeze
Over my hair, and tracing my brows,
Till I knew you not from a little wind:
—I wonder now if God allows
      Us only one moment his keys.

      If only then
You could have unlocked the moon on the night,
And I baptized myself in the light
Of your love; we both have entered then the white
      Pure passion, and never again.

      I wonder if only
You had taken me then, how different
Life would have been: should I have spent
Myself in waste, and you have bent
      Your pride, through being lonely?

                                    D.H. LAWRENCE

IX

Bei Hennef

The little river twittering in the twilight,
The wan, wondering look of the pale sky,
        This is almost bliss.

And everything shut up and gone to sleep,
All the troubles and anxieties and pain
        Gone under the twilight.

Only the twilight now, and the soft "Sh!" of the river
        That will last for ever.

And at last I know my love for you is here,
I can see it all, it is whole like the twilight,
It is large, so large, I could not see it before
Because of the little lights and flickers and interruptions,
        Troubles, anxieties and pains.

        You are the call and I am the answer,
        You are the wish, and I the fulfilment,
        You are the night, and I the day.
                What else—it is perfect enough,
                It is perfectly complete,
                You and I,
                What more—?
Strange, how we suffer in spite of this!

X

LIGHTNING

I felt the lurch and halt of her heart
     Next my breast, where my own heart was beating;
And I laughed to feel it plunge and bound,
And strange in my blood-swept ears was the sound
     Of the words I kept repeating,
Repeating with tightened arms, and the hot blood's blindfold art.

Her breath flew warm against my neck,
     Warm as a flame in the close night air;
And the sense of her clinging flesh was sweet
Where her arms and my neck's blood-surge could meet.
     Holding her thus, did I care
That the black night hid her from me, blotted out every speck?

I leaned me forward to find her lips,
     And claim her utterly in a kiss,
When the lightning flew across her face,
And I saw her for the flaring space
     Of a second, afraid of the clips
Of my arms, inert with dread, wilted in fear of my kiss.

A moment, like a wavering spark,
     Her face lay there before my breast,
Pale love lost in a snow of fear,
And guarded by a glittering tear,
     And lips apart with dumb cries;
A moment, and she was taken again in the merciful dark.

I heard the thunder, and felt the rain,
     And my arms fell loose, and I was dumb.
Almost I hated her, she was so good,
Hated myself, and the place, and my blood,
     Which burned with rage, as I bade her come
Home, away home, ere the lightning floated forth again.

               D.H. LAWRENCE

XI

Song-Day in Autumn

When the autumn roses
    Are heavy with dew,
Before the mist discloses
    The leaf's brown hue,
You would, among the laughing hills
    Of yesterday
Walk innocent in the daffodils,
Coiffing up your auburn hair
In a puritan fillet, a chaste white snare
To catch and keep me with you there
    So far away.

When from the autumn roses
    Trickles the dew,
When the blue mist uncloses
    And the sun looks through,
You from those startled hills
    Come away,
Out of the withering daffodils;
Thoughtful, and half afraid,
Plaiting a heavy, auburn braid
And coiling it round the wise brows of a maid
    Who was scared in her play.

When in the autumn roses
    Creeps a bee,
And a trembling flower encloses
    His ecstasy,
You from your lonely walk
    Turn away,
And leaning to me like a flower on its stalk,
Wait among the beeches

For your late bee who beseeches
To creep through your loosened hair till he reaches,
    Your heart of dismay.

XII

Aware

Slowly the moon is rising out of the ruddy haze,
Divesting herself of her golden shift, and so
Emerging white and exquisite; and I in amaze
See in the sky before me, a woman I did not know
I loved, but there she goes and her beauty hurts my heart;
I follow her down the night, begging her not to depart.

XIII

A Pang of Reminiscence

High and smaller goes the moon, she is small and very far from me,
Wistful and candid, watching me wistfully, and I see
Trembling blue in her pallor a tear that surely I have seen before,
A tear which I had hoped that even hell held not again in store.

XIV

A White Blossom

A tiny moon as white and small as a single jasmine flower
Leans all alone above my window, on night's wintry bower,
Liquid as lime-tree blossom, soft as brilliant water or rain
She shines, the one white love of my youth, which all sin cannot stain.

XV

Red Moon-Rise

The train in running across the weald has fallen into a steadier stroke
So even, it beats like silence, and sky and earth in one unbroke
Embrace of darkness lie around, and crushed between them all the
    loose
And littered lettering of leaves and hills and houses closed, and
    we can use
The open book of landscape no more, for the covers of darkness have
    shut upon
Its written pages, and sky and earth and all between are closed in one.

And we are smothered between the darkness, we close our eyes and say
    "Hush!" we try
To escape in sleep the terror of this immense deep darkness, and we lie
Wrapped up for sleep. And then, dear God, from out of the twofold
    darkness, red
As if from the womb the moon arises, as if the twin-walled darkness
    had bled
In one great spasm of birth and given us this new, red moon-rise
Which lies on the knees of the darkness bloody, and makes us hide our
    eyes.

The train beats frantic in haste, and struggles away
From this ruddy terror of birth that has slid down
From out of the loins of night to flame our way
With fear; but God, I am glad, so glad that I drown
My terror with joy of confirmation, for now
Lies God all red before me, and I am glad,
As the Magi were when they saw the rosy brow
Of the Infant bless their constant folly which had
Brought them thither to God: for now I know
That the Womb is a great red passion whence rises all
The shapeliness that decks us here-below:
Yea like the fire that boils within this ball

Of earth, and quickens all herself with flowers,
God burns within the stiffened clay of us;
And every flash of thought that we and ours
Send up to heaven, and every movement, does
Fly like a spark from this God-fire of passion;
And pain of birth, and joy of the begetting,
And sweat of labour, and the meanest fashion
Of fretting or of gladness, but the jetting
Of a trail of the great fire against the sky
Where we can see it, a jet from the innermost fire:
And even in the watery shells that lie
Alive within the cozy under-mire,
A grain of this same fire I can descry.

And then within the screaming birds that fly
Across the lightning when the storm leaps higher;
And then the swirling, flaming folk that try
To come like fire-flames at their fierce desire,
They are as earth's dread, spurting flames that ply
Awhile and gush forth death and then expire.
And though it be love's wet blue eyes that cry
To hot love to relinquish its desire,
Still in their depths I see the same red spark
As rose to-night upon us from the dark.

RETURN

Now I am come again, you who have so desired
My coming, why do you look away from me?
Why does your cheek burn against me—have I inspired
Such anger as sets your mouth unwontedly?

Ah, here I sit while you break the music beneath
Your bow; for broken it is, and hurting to hear:
Cease then from music—does anguish of absence bequeath
Me only aloofness when I would draw near?

XVII

The Appeal

You, Helen, who see the stars
As mistletoe berries burning in a black tree,
You surely, seeing I am a bowl of kisses,
Should put your mouth to mine and drink of me.

Helen, you let my kisses steam
Wasteful into the night's black nostrils; drink
Me up I pray; oh you who are Night's Bacchante,
How can you from my bowl of kisses shrink!

XVIII

REPULSED

The last, silk-floating thought has gone from the dandelion stem,
And the flesh of the stalk holds up for nothing a blank diadem.

The night's flood-winds have lifted my last desire from me,
And my hollow flesh stands up in the night abandonedly.

As I stand on this hill, with the whitening cave of the city beyond,
Helen, I am despoiled of my pride, and my soul turns fond:

Overhead the nightly heavens like an open, immense eye,
Like a cat's distended pupil sparkles with sudden stars,
As with thoughts that flash and crackle in uncouth malignancy
They glitter at me, and I fear the fierce snapping of night's
thought-stars.

Beyond me, up the darkness, goes the gush of the lights of two
    towns,
As the breath which rushes upwards from the nostrils of an
    immense
Life crouched across the globe, ready, if need be, to pounce
Across the space upon heaven's high hostile eminence.

All round me, but far away, the night's twin consciousness roars
With sounds that endlessly swell and sink like the storm of thought
in the brain,
Lifting and falling like slow breaths taken, pulsing like oars
Immense that beat the blood of the night down its vein.

The night is immense and awful, Helen, and I am insect small
In the fur of this hill, clung on to the fur of shaggy, black heather.
A palpitant speck in the fur of the night, and afraid of all,
Seeing the world and the sky like creatures hostile together.

And I in the fur of the world, and you a pale fleck from the sky,
How we hate each other to-night, hate, you and I,
As the world of activity hates the dream that goes on on high,
As a man hates the dreaming woman he loves, but who will not reply.

XIX

DREAM-CONFUSED

Is that the moon
At the window so big and red?
No one in the room,
No one near the bed—?

Listen, her shoon
Palpitating down the stair?
—Or a beat of wings at the window there?

A moment ago
She kissed me warm on the mouth,
The very moon in the south
Is warm with a bloody glow,
The moon from far abysses
Signalling those two kisses.

And now the moon
Goes slowly out of the west,
And slowly back in my breast
My kisses are sinking, soon
To leave me at rest.

Corot

The trees rise tall and taller, lifted
On a subtle rush of cool grey flame
That issuing out of the dawn has sifted
    The spirit from each leaf's frame.

For the trailing, leisurely rapture of life
Drifts dimly forward, easily hidden
By bright leaves uttered aloud, and strife
    Of shapes in the grey mist chidden.

The grey, phosphorescent, pellucid advance
Of the luminous purpose of God, shines out
Where the lofty trees athwart stream chance
    To shake flakes of its shadow about.

The subtle, steady rush of the whole
Grey foam-mist of advancing God,
As He silently sweeps to His somewhere, his goal,
    Is heard in the grass of the sod.

Is heard in the windless whisper of leaves
In the silent labours of men in the fields,
In the downward dropping of flimsy sheaves
    Of cloud the rain skies yield.

In the tapping haste of a fallen leaf,
In the flapping of red-roof smoke, and the small
Foot-stepping tap of men beneath
    These trees so huge and tall.

For what can all sharp-rimmed substance but catch
In a backward ripple, God's purpose, reveal
For a moment His mighty direction, snatch
    A spark beneath His wheel.

Since God sweeps onward dim and vast,
Creating the channelled vein of Man
And Leaf for His passage, His shadow is cast
     On all for us to scan.

Ah listen, for Silence is not lonely:
Imitate the magnificent trees
That speak no word of their rapture, but only
     Breathe largely the luminous breeze.

Morning Work

A gang of labourers on the piled wet timber
That shines blood-red beside the railway siding
Seem to be making out of the blue of the morning
Something faery and fine, the shuttles sliding,

The red-gold spools of their hands and faces shuttling
Hither and thither across the morn's crystalline frame
Of blue: trolls at the cave of ringing cerulean mining,
And laughing with work, living their work like a game.

XXII

Transformations

I

The Town

Oh you stiff shapes, swift transformation seethes
About you: only last night you were
A Sodom smouldering in the dense, soiled air;
To-day a thicket of sunshine with blue smoke-wreaths.

To-morrow swimming in evening's vague, dim vapour
Like a weeded city in shadow under the sea,
Beneath an ocean of shimmering light you will be:
Then a group of toadstools waiting the moon's white taper.

And when I awake in the morning, after rain,
To find the new houses a cluster of lilies glittering
In scarlet, alive with the birds' bright twittering,
I'll say your bond of ugliness is vain.

II

The Earth

Oh Earth, you spinning clod of earth,
And then you lamp, you lemon-coloured beauty;
Oh Earth, you rotten apple rolling downward,
Then brilliant Earth, from the burr of night in beauty
As a jewel-brown horse-chestnut newly issued:—
You are all these, and strange, it is my duty
To take you all, sordid or radiant tissued.

III

Men

Oh labourers, oh shuttles across the blue frame of morning,
You feet of the rainbow balancing the sky!
Oh you who flash your arms like rockets to heaven,
Who in lassitude lean as yachts on the sea-wind lie!
You who in crowds are rhododendrons in blossom,
Who stand alone in pride like lighted lamps;
Who grappling down with work or hate or passion,
Take strange lithe form of a beast that sweats and ramps:
You who are twisted in grief like crumpled beech-leaves,
Who curl in sleep like kittens, who kiss as a swarm
Of clustered, vibrating bees; who fall to earth
At last like a bean-pod: what are you, oh multiform?

XXIII

Renascence

We have bit no forbidden apple,
     Eve and I,
Yet the splashes of day and night
Falling round us no longer dapple
The same Eden with purple and white.

This is our own still valley
     Our Eden, our home,
But day shows it vivid with feeling
And the pallor of night does not tally
With dark sleep that once covered its ceiling.

My little red heifer, to-night I looked in her eyes,
     —She will calve to-morrow:
Last night when I went with the lantern, the sow was grabbing her
    litter
With red, snarling jaws: and I heard the cries
Of the new-born, and after that, the old owl, then the bats that
    flitter.

And I woke to the sound of the wood-pigeons, and lay and
    listened,
     Till I could borrow
A few quick beats of a wood-pigeon's heart, and when I did rise
The morning sun on the shaken iris glistened,
And I saw that home, this valley, was wider than Paradise.

I learned it all from my Eve
     This warm, dumb wisdom.
She's a finer instructress than years;
She has taught my heart-strings to weave
Through the web of all laughter and tears.

And now I see the valley
　　　Fleshed all like me
With feelings that change and quiver:
And all things seem to tally
　　　With something in me,
Something of which she's the giver.

XXIV

Dog-Tired

If she would come to me here,
        Now the sunken swaths
        Are glittering paths
To the sun, and the swallows cut clear
Into the low sun—if she came to me here!

If she would come to me now,
Before the last mown harebells are dead,
While that vetch clump yet burns red;
Before all the bats have dropped from the bough
Into the cool of night—if she came to me now!

The horses are untackled, the chattering machine
Is still at last. If she would come,
I would gather up the warm hay from
The hill-brow, and lie in her lap till the green
Sky ceased to quiver, and lost its tired sheen.

I should like to drop
On the hay, with my head on her knee
And lie stone still, while she
Breathed quiet above me—we could stop
Till the stars came out to see.

I should like to lie still
As if I was dead—but feeling
Her hand go stealing
Over my face and my hair until
This ache was shed.

D.H. LAWRENCE

XXV

Michael-Angelo

God shook thy roundness in His finger's cup,
He sunk His hands in firmness down thy sides,
And drew the circle of His grasp, O Man,
Along thy limbs delighted, thine, His bride's.

And so thou wert God-shapen: His finger
Curved thy mouth for thee, and His strong shoulder
Planted thee upright: art not proud to see
In the curve of thine exquisite form the joy of the Moulder?

He took a handful of light and rolled a ball,
Compressed it till its beam grew wondrous dark,
Then gave thee thy dark eyes, O Man, that all
He made had doorway to thee through that spark.

God, lonely, put down His mouth in a kiss of creation,
He kissed thee, O Man, in a passion of love, and left
The vivid life of His love in thy mouth and thy nostrils;
Keep then the kiss from the adultress' theft.

DIALECT POEMS

I

Violets

Sister, tha knows while we was on the planks
    Aside o' th' grave, while th' coffin wor lyin' yet
On th' yaller clay, an' th' white flowers top of it
    Tryin' to keep off 'n him a bit o' th' wet,

An' parson makin' haste, an' a' the black
    Huddlin' close together a cause o' th' rain,
Did t' 'appen ter notice a bit of a lass away back
    By a head-stun, sobbin' an' sobbin' again?

      —How should I be lookin' round
        An' me standin' on the plank
      Beside the open ground,
        Where our Ted 'ud soon be sank?

      Yi, an' 'im that young,
        Snapped sudden out of all
      His wickedness, among
        Pals worse n'r ony name as you could call.

Let be that; there's some o' th' bad as we
    Like better nor all your good, an' 'e was one.
—An' cos I liked him best, yi, bett'r nor thee,
    I canna bide to think where he is gone.

Ah know tha liked 'im bett'r nor me. But let
    Me tell thee about this lass. When you had gone
Ah stopped behind on t' pad i' th' drippin wet
    An' watched what 'er 'ad on.

Tha should ha' seed her slive up when we'd gone,
    Tha should ha' seed her kneel an' look in
At th' sloppy wet grave—an' 'er little neck shone
    That white, an' 'er shook that much, I'd like to begin

Scraïghtin' my-sen as well. 'En undid her black
    Jacket at th' bosom, an' took from out of it
Over a double 'andful of violets, all in a pack
    Ravelled blue and white—warm, for a bit

O' th' smell come waftin' to me. 'Er put 'er face
    Right intil 'em and scraïghted out again,
Then after a bit 'er dropped 'em down that place,
    An' I come away, because o' the teemin' rain.

II

WHETHER OR NOT

I

Dunna thee tell me its his'n, mother,
      Dunna thee, dunna thee.
—Oh ay! he'll be comin' to tell thee his-sèn
      Wench, wunna he?

Tha doesna mean to say to me, mother,
      He's gone wi that—
—My gel, owt'll do for a man i' the dark,
      Tha's got it flat.

But 'er's old, mother, 'er's twenty year
      Older nor him—
—Ay, an' yaller as a crowflower, an' yet i' the dark
      Er'd do for Tim.

Tha niver believes it, mother, does ter?
      It's somebody's lies.
—Ax him thy-sèn wench—a widder's lodger;
      It's no surprise.

II

A widow of forty-five
With a bitter, swarthy skin,
To ha' 'ticed a lad o' twenty-five
An' 'im to have been took in!

A widow of forty-five
As has sludged like a horse all her life,
Till 'er's tough as whit-leather, to slive
Atween a lad an' 'is wife!

A widow of forty-five.
A tough old otchel wi' long
Witch teeth, an' 'er black hawk-eyes as I've
Mistrusted all along!

An' me as 'as kep my-sen
Shut like a daisy bud,
Clean an' new an' nice, so's when
He wed he'd ha'e summat good!

An' 'im as nice an' fresh
As any man i' the force,
To ha'e gone an' given his white young flesh
To a woman that coarse!

III

You're stout to brave this snow, Miss Stainwright,
  Are you makin' Brinsley way?
—I'm off up th' line to Underwood
  Wi' a dress as is wanted to-day.

Oh are you goin' to Underwood?
  'Appen then you've 'eered?
—What's that as 'appen I've 'eered-on, Missis,
  Speak up, you nedna be feared.

Why, your young man an' Widow Naylor,
  Her as he lodges wi',
They say he's got her wi' childt; but there,
  It's nothing to do wi' me.

Though if it's true they'll turn him out
  O' th' p'lice force, without fail;
An' if it's not true, I'd back my life
  They'll listen to *her* tale.

Well, I'm believin' no tale, Missis,
  I'm seein' for my-sen;

An' when I know for sure, Missis,
  I'll talk *then*.

IV

Nay robin red-breast, tha nedna
  Sit noddin' thy head at me;
My breast's as red as thine, I reckon,
  Flayed red, if tha could but see.

Nay, you blessed pee-whips,
  You nedna screet at me!
I'm screetin' my-sen, but are-na goin'
  To let iv'rybody see.

Tha *art* smock-ravelled, bunny,
  Larropin' neck an' crop
I' th' snow: but I's warrant thee, bunny,
  I'm further ower th' top.

V

Now sithee theer at th' railroad crossin'
Warmin' his-sen at the stool o' fire
Under the tank as fills the ingines,
If there isn't my dearly-beloved liar!

My constable wi' 'is buttoned breast
As stout as the truth, my sirs!—An' 'is face
As bold as a robin! It's much he cares
For this nice old shame and disgrace.

Oh but he drops his flag when 'e sees me,
Yes, an' 'is face goes white. . . oh yes
Tha can stare at me wi' thy fierce blue eyes,
But tha doesna stare me out, I guess!

VI

Whativer brings thee out so far
    In a' this depth o' snow?
—I'm takin' 'ome a weddin' dress
    If tha maun know.

Why, is there a weddin' at Underwood,
    As tha ne'd trudge up here?
—It's Widow Naylor's weddin'-dress,
    An' 'er's wantin it, I hear.

'Er doesna want no weddin-dress. . .
    What—but what dost mean?
—Doesn't ter know what I mean, Tim?—Yi,
    Tha must' a' been hard to wean!

Tha'rt a good-un at suckin-in yet, Timmy;
    But tell me, isn't it true
As 'er'll be wantin' *my* weddin' dress
    In a week or two?

Tha's no occasions ter ha'e me on
    Lizzie—what's done is done!
—*Done*, I should think so—Done! But might
    I ask when tha begun?

It's thee as 'as done it as much as me,
    Lizzie, I tell thee that.
—"Me gotten a childt to thy landlady—!"
    Tha's gotten thy answer pat,

As tha allers hast—but let me tell thee
    Hasna ter sent me whoam, when I
Was a'most burstin' mad o' my-sen
    An' walkin' in agony;

After thy kisses, Lizzie, after
    Tha's lain right up to me Lizzie, an' melted

Into me, melted into me, Lizzie,
      Till I was verily swelted.

An' if my landlady seed me like it,
      An' if 'er clawkin', tiger's eyes
Went through me just as the light went out
      Is it any cause for surprise?

No cause for surprise at all, my lad,
      After lickin' and snuffin' at me, tha could
Turn thy mouth on a woman like her—
      Did ter find her good?

Ay, I did, but afterwards
      I should like to ha' killed her!
—Afterwards!—an' after how long
      Wor it tha'd liked to 'a killed her?

Say no more, Liz, dunna thee,
      I might lose my-sen.
—I'll only say good-bye to thee, Timothy,
      An' gi'e her thee back again.

I'll ta'e thy word 'Good-bye,' Liz,
      But I shonna marry her,
I shonna for nobody.—It is
      Very nice on you, Sir.

The childt maun ta'e its luck, it maun,
      An' she maun ta'e *her* luck,
For I tell ye I shonna marry her—
      What her's got, her took.

That's spoken like a man, Timmy,
      That's spoken like a man. . .
"He up an' fired off his pistol
      An' then away he ran."

I damn well shanna marry 'er,
        So chew at it no more,
Or I'll chuck the flamin' lot of you—
        —You nedn't have swore.

VII

That's his collar round the candle-stick
An' that's the dark blue tie I bought 'im,
An' these is the woman's kids he's so fond on,
An' 'ere comes the cat that caught 'im.

I dunno where his eyes was—a gret
Round-shouldered hag! My sirs, to think
Of him stoopin' to her! You'd wonder he could
Throw hisself in that sink.

I expect you know who I am, Mrs Naylor!
        —Who yer are?—yis, you're Lizzie Stainwright.
'An 'appen you might guess what I've come for?
        —'Appen I mightn't, 'appen I might.

You knowed as I was courtin' Tim Merfin.
        —Yis, I knowed 'e wor courtin' thee.
An' yet you've been carryin' on wi' him.
        —Ay, an' 'im wi' me.

Well, now you've got to pay for it,
        —An' if I han, what's that to thee?
For 'e isn't goin' to marry you.
        —Is it a toss-up 'twixt thee an' me?

It's no toss-up 'twixt thee an' me.
        —Then what art colleyfoglin' for?
I'm not havin' your orts an' slarts.
        —Which on us said you wor?

I want you to know 'e's non *marryin'* you.
        —Tha wants 'im thy-sen too bad.

Though I'll see as 'e pays you, an' comes to the scratch.
    —Tha'rt for doin' a lot wi' th' lad.

VIII

To think I should ha'e to haffle an' caffle
    Wi' a woman, an' pay 'er a price
For lettin' me marry the lad as I thought
    To marry wi' cabs an' rice.

But we'll go unbeknown to the registrar,
    An' give *'er* what money there is,
For I won't be beholden to such as her
    For anythink of his.

IX

Take off thy duty stripes, Tim,
    An' come wi' me in here,
Ta'e off thy p'lice-man's helmet
    An' look me clear.

I wish tha hadna done it, Tim,
    I do, an' that I do!
For whenever I look thee i' th' face, I s'll see
    Her face too.

I wish tha could wesh 'er off'n thee,
    For I used to think that thy
Face was the finest thing that iver
    Met my eye. . .

X

Twenty pound o' thy own tha hast, and fifty pound ha'e I,
Thine shall go to pay the woman, an' wi' my bit we'll buy
All as we shall want for furniture when tha leaves this place,
An' we'll be married at th' registrar—now lift thy face.

Lift thy face an' look at me, man, up an' look at me:
Sorry I am for this business, an' sorry if I ha'e driven thee
To such a thing: but it's a poor tale, that I'm bound to say,
Before I can ta'e thee I've got a widow of forty-five to pay.

Dunnat thee think but what I love thee—I love thee well,
But 'deed an' I wish as this tale o' thine wor niver my tale to tell;
Deed an' I wish as I could stood at the altar wi' thee an' been proud
    o' thee,
That I could ha' been first woman to thee, as thou'rt first man to me.

But we maun ma'e the best on't—I'll rear thy childt if 'er'll yield
    it to me,
An' then wi' that twenty pound we gi'e 'er I s'd think 'er wunna be
So very much worser off than 'er wor before—An' now look up
An' answer me—for I've said my say, an' there's no more sorrow to sup.

Yi, tha'rt a man, tha'rt a fine big man, but niver a baby had eyes
As sulky an' ormin' as thine. Hast owt to say otherwise
From what I've arranged wi' thee? Eh man, what a stubborn jackass
    thou art,
Kiss me then—there!—ne'er mind if I scraight—I wor fond o' thee,
    Sweetheart.

III

A Collier's Wife

Somebody's knocking at the door
      Mother, come down and see.
—I's think it's nobbut a beggar,
      Say, I'm busy.

Its not a beggar, mother,—hark
      How hard he knocks. . .
—Eh, tha'rt a mard-'arsed kid,
      'E'll gi'e thee socks!

Shout an' ax what 'e wants,
      I canna come down.
—'E says "Is it Arthur Holliday's?"
      Say "Yes," tha clown.

'E says, "Tell your mother as 'er mester's
      Got hurt i' th' pit."
What—oh my sirs, 'e never says that,
      That's niver it.

Come out o' the way an' let me see,
      Eh, there's no peace!
An' stop thy scraightin', childt,
      Do shut thy face.

"Your mester's 'ad an accident,
      An' they're ta'ein 'im i' th' ambulance
To Nottingham,"—Eh dear o' me
      If 'e's not a man for mischance!

Wheers he hurt this time, lad?
      —I dunna know,
They on'y towd me it wor bad—
      It would be so!

Eh, what a man!—an' that cobbly road,
        They'll jolt him a'most to death,
I'm sure he's in for some trouble
        Nigh every time he takes breath.

Out o' my way, childt—dear o' me, wheer
        Have I put his clean stockings and shirt;
Goodness knows if they'll be able
        To take off his pit dirt.

An' what a moan he'll make—there niver
        Was such a man for a fuss
If anything ailed him—at any rate
        I shan't have him to nuss.

I do hope it's not very bad!
        Eh, what a shame it seems
As some should ha'e hardly a smite o' trouble
        An' others has reams.

It's a shame as 'e should be knocked about
        Like this, I'm sure it is!
He's had twenty accidents, if he's had one;
        Owt bad, an' it's his.

There's one thing, we'll have peace for a bit,
        Thank Heaven for a peaceful house;
An' there's compensation, sin' it's accident,
        An' club money—I nedn't grouse.

An' a fork an' a spoon he'll want, an' what else;
        I s'll never catch that train—
What a trapse it is if a man gets hurt—
        I s'd think he'll get right again.

IV

THE DRAINED CUP

The snow is witherin' off'n th' gress
       Love, should I tell thee summat?
The snow is witherin' off'n th' gress
An' a thick mist sucks at the clots o' snow,
An' the moon above in a weddin' dress
Goes fogged an' slow—
       Love, should I tell thee summat?

Tha's been snowed up i' this cottage wi' me,
       Nay, I'm tellin' thee summat.—
Tha's bin snowed up i' this cottage wi' me
While th' clocks has a' run down an' stopped
An' the short days withering silently
Unbeknown have dropped.
       —Yea, but I'm tellin' thee summat.

How many days dost think has gone?—
       Now I'm tellin' thee summat.
How many days dost think has gone?
How many days has the candle-light shone
On us as tha got more white an' wan?
—Seven days, or none—
       Am I not tellin' thee summat?

Tha come to bid farewell to me—
       Tha'rt frit o' summat.
To kiss me and shed a tear wi' me,
Then off and away wi' the weddin' ring
For the girl who was grander, and better than me
For marrying—
       Tha'rt frit o' summat?

I durstna kiss thee tha trembles so,
  Tha'rt frit o' summat.
Tha arena very flig to go,
'Appen the mist from the thawin' snow
Daunts thee—it isna for love, I know,
That tha'rt loath to go.
  —Dear o' me, say summat.

Maun tha cling to the wa' as tha goes,
  So bad as that?
Tha'lt niver get into thy weddin' clothes
At that rate—eh, theer goes thy hat;
Ne'er mind, good-bye lad, now I lose
My joy, God knows,
  —An' worse nor that.

The road goes under the apple tree;
  Look, for I'm showin' thee summat.
An' if it worn't for the mist, tha'd see
The great black wood on all sides o' thee
Wi' the little pads going cunningly
To ravel thee.
  So listen, I'm tellin' thee summat.

When tha comes to the beechen avenue,
  I'm warnin' thee o' summat.
Mind tha shall keep inwards, a few
Steps to the right, for the gravel pits
Are steep an' deep wi' watter, an' you
Are scarce o' your wits.
  Remember, I've warned the o' summat.

An' mind when crossin' the planken bridge,
  Again I warn ye o' summat.
Ye slip not on the slippery ridge
Of the thawin' snow, or it'll be
A long put-back to your gran' marridge,
I'm tellin' ye.
  Nay, are ter scared o' summat?

In kep the thick black curtains drawn,
        Am I not tellin' thee summat?
Against the knockin' of sevenfold dawn,
An' red-tipped candles from morn to morn
Have dipped an' danced upon thy brawn
Till thou art worn—
        Oh, I have cost thee summat.

Look in the mirror an' see thy-sen,
        —What, I am showin' thee summat.
Wasted an' wan tha sees thy-sen,
An' thy hand that holds the mirror shakes
Till tha drops the glass and tha shudders when
Thy luck breaks.
        Sure, tha'rt afraid o' summat.

Frail thou art, my saucy man,
        —Listen, I'm tellin' thee summat.
Tottering and tired thou art, my man,
Tha came to say good-bye to me,
An' tha's done it so well, that now I can
Part wi' thee.
        —Master, I'm givin' thee summat.

THE SCHOOLMASTER

I

A Snowy Day in School

All the slow school hours, round the irregular hum of the class,
Have pressed immeasurable spaces of hoarse silence
Muffling my mind, as snow muffles the sounds that pass
Down the soiled street. We have pattered the lessons ceaselessly—

But the faces of the boys, in the brooding, yellow light
Have shone for me like a crowded constellation of stars,
Like full-blown flowers dimly shaking at the night,
Like floating froth on an ebbing shore in the moon.

Out of each star, dark, strange beams that disquiet:
In the open depths of each flower, dark restless drops:
Twin bubbles, shadow-full of mystery and challenge in the foam's
    whispering riot:
—How can I answer the challenge of so many eyes!

The thick snow is crumpled on the roof, it plunges down
Awfully. Must I call back those hundred eyes?—A voice
Wakes from the hum, faltering about a noun—
My question! My God, I must break from this hoarse silence

That rustles beyond the stars to me.—There,
I have startled a hundred eyes, and I must look
Them an answer back. It is more than I can bear.

The snow descends as if the dull sky shook
In flakes of shadow down; and through the gap
Between the ruddy schools sweeps one black rook.

The rough snowball in the playground stands huge and still
With fair flakes settling down on it.—Beyond, the town
Is lost in the shadowed silence the skies distil.

And all things are possessed by silence, and they can brood
Wrapped up in the sky's dim space of hoarse silence
Earnestly—and oh for me this class is a bitter rood.

II

The Best of School

The blinds are drawn because of the sun,
And the boys and the room in a colourless gloom
Of under-water float: bright ripples run
Across the walls as the blinds are blown
To let the sunlight in; and I,
As I sit on the beach of the class alone,
Watch the boys in their summer blouses,
As they write, their round heads busily bowed:
And one after another rouses
And lifts his face and looks at me,
And my eyes meet his very quietly,
Then he turns again to his work, with glee.

With glee he turns, with a little glad
Ecstasy of work he turns from me,
An ecstasy surely sweet to be had.
And very sweet while the sunlight waves
In the fresh of the morning, it is to be
A teacher of these young boys, my slaves
Only as swallows are slaves to the eaves
They build upon, as mice are slaves
To the man who threshes and sows the sheaves.

Oh, sweet it is
To feel the lads' looks light on me,
Then back in a swift, bright flutter to work,
As birds who are stealing turn and flee.

Touch after touch I feel on me
As their eyes glance at me for the grain
Of rigour they taste delightedly.

                                        And all the class,
          As tendrils reached out yearningly
          Slowly rotate till they touch the tree
          That they cleave unto, that they leap along
          Up to their lives—so they to me.

          So do they cleave and cling to me,
          So I lead them up, so do they twine
          Me up, caress and clothe with free
          Fine foliage of lives this life of mine;
          The lowest stem of this life of mine,
          The old hard stem of my life
          That bears aloft towards rarer skies
          My top of life, that buds on high
          Amid the high wind's enterprise.
          They all do clothe my ungrowing life
          With a rich, a thrilled young clasp of life;
          A clutch of attachment, like parenthood,
          Mounts up to my heart, and I find it good.

And I lift my head upon the troubled tangled world, and though the
     pain
Of living my life were doubled, I still have this to comfort and
     sustain,
I have such swarming sense of lives at the base of me, such sense of
     lives
Clustering upon me, reaching up, as each after the other strives
To follow my life aloft to the fine wild air of life and the storm of
     thought,
And though I scarcely see the boys, or know that they are there,
     distraught
As I am with living my life in earnestness, still progressively and
     alone,
Though they cling, forgotten the most part, not companions, scarcely
     known
To me—yet still because of the sense of their closeness clinging
     densely to me,
And slowly fingering up my stem and following all tinily
The way that I have gone and now am leading, they are dear to me.

They keep me assured, and when my soul feels lonely,
All mistrustful of thrusting its shoots where only
I alone am living, then it keeps
Me comforted to feel the warmth that creeps
Up dimly from their striving; it heartens my strife:
And when my heart is chill with loneliness,
Then comforts it the creeping tenderness
Of all the strays of life that climb my life.

AFTERNOON IN SCHOOL

The Last Lesson

When will the bell ring, and end this weariness?
How long have they tugged the leash, and strained apart
My pack of unruly hounds: I cannot start
Them again on a quarry of knowledge they hate to hunt,
I can haul them and urge them no more.
No more can I endure to bear the brunt
Of the books that lie out on the desks: a full three score
Of several insults of blotted page and scrawl
Of slovenly work that they have offered me.
I am sick, and tired more than any thrall
Upon the woodstacks working weariedly.

                         And shall I take
The last dear fuel and heap it on my soul
Till I rouse my will like a fire to consume
Their dross of indifference, and burn the scroll
Of their insults in punishment?—I will not!
I will not waste myself to embers for them,
Not all for them shall the fires of my life be hot,
For myself a heap of ashes of weariness, till sleep
Shall have raked the embers clear: I will keep
Some of my strength for myself, for if I should sell
It all for them, I should hate them—
                    —I will sit and wait for the bell.

A Note About the Author

David Herbert Lawrence (1885–1930), more commonly known as D.H. Lawrence, was a British writer and poet often surrounded by controversy. His works explored issues of sexuality, emotional health, masculinity, and reflected on the dehumanizing effects of industrialization. Lawrence's opinions acquired him many enemies, censorship, and prosecution. Because of this, he lived the majority of his second half of life in a self-imposed exile. Despite the controversy and criticism, he posthumously was championed for his artistic integrity and moral severity.

A Note from the Publisher

Spanning many genres, from non-fiction essays to literature classics to children's books and lyric poetry, Mint Edition books showcase the master works of our time in a modern new package. The text is freshly typeset, is clean and easy to read, and features a new note about the author in each volume. Many books also include exclusive new introductory material. Every book boasts a striking new cover, which makes it as appropriate for collecting as it is for gift giving. Mint Edition books are only printed when a reader orders them, so natural resources are not wasted. We're proud that our books are never manufactured in excess and exist only in the exact quantity they need to be read and enjoyed.

bookfinity™

Discover more of your favorite classics with Bookfinity™.

- Track your reading with custom book lists.
- Get great book recommendations for your personalized Reader Type.
- Add reviews for your favorite books.
- AND MUCH MORE!

Visit **bookfinity.com** and take the fun Reader Type quiz to get started.

Enjoy our classic and modern companion pairings!

Classic & Modern